7

UTRILLO

MONTMARTRE

THE LITTLE LIBRARY
OF ART

FIRST PUBLISHED 1957
REPRINTED FOUR TIMES
REPRINTED 1961
1.6.

CATALOGUE NO. 5920/U

UTRILLO

MONTMARTRE

BY

JEAN OBERLÉ

METHUEN AND CO. LTD

36 ESSEX STREET · STRAND · LONDON WC2

Maurice Utrillo was born in Montmartre in 1883. Montmartre at that time was still a village centred around its little church—the oldest church in Paris. Hens scratched about among the uneven paving-stones of the streets, cows chewed the cud quietly in the stables of the old farmhouses, and on the "Butte"—the hill of Montmartre—"they hadn't started Sacred-hearting", to translate the words of a verse-maker of the day; in other words, the white domes of the neo-byzantine basilica of the Sacré-Cœur were still part of a grandiose project on an architect's table. That was the Montmartre of the late nineteenth century—quiet and peaceful, with its little population of village folk and artisans who rarely "went down" to the city. The city in those days lay on the other side of the "outer boulevard", by which name the Parisians designated the Boulevard de Clichy, the site of the Moulin Rouge, or the Boulevard de Rochechouart where the Élysée-Montmartre stood.

Montmartre, with its serenity, its airy elevation, its light and its gardens, was a paradise for artists, and many a poet and painter chose to

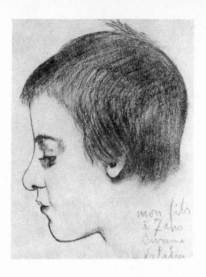

UTRILLO AT THE AGE OF SEVEN,
BY VALADON. 1891.

work there far from the bustle of the city. Ziem, who had his studio in the Rue Lepic, painted his "Souvenirs of Venice" there from one year's end to the next. Renoir had a studio in the Rue Cortot, and painted the Moulin Rouge which was just next door. Claude Monet and many another impressionist had only to set up their easels in their gardens to paint their "open air" studies.

Utrillo was the natural child of Suzanne Valadon, a beautiful young woman who lived by her talent as an acrobat or by posing as a model for artists—among them Puvis de Chavannes, Degas and Renoir—before becoming a painter herself. Utrillo always held his mother in great veneration, although their life together was not without its stormy passages. His first canvases he signed Maurice Utrillo-Valadon or Maurice Utrillo-V. As for his father, no one, perhaps not even Suzanne Valadon herself, knew who he was. The only father the boy knew was a Spaniard called Utrillo who lived on the Butte Montmartre and who offered to adopt the son of Suzanne Valadon before the law and under his own name.

For the seventy-two years of his life Maurice Utrillo was dogged by misfortune. From his unhappy ancestry he inherited a taste for drink which became an addiction, and which left its mark on both his personality and his reason. A deeply sensitive and original artist, always living on the outer margins of society, Utrillo never escaped, even in his youth, the torment of the demon within him. "Artiste maudit" he has often been called, thus placing him in the company of those other artists whose lives were lived under a curse—Van Gogh, Gauguin, and even Toulouse-Lautrec. Yet there is in the genius of Utrillo something profoundly fresh and delicate, and even his paintings of the most squalid back streets or of those wretched, tumble-down old houses are often touched with a freshness and childlike innocence that has no equal.

Utrillo is an outdoor artist. All his life he painted outdoor scenes, almost always the same size—about 32 inches across—and almost

PLACE DU TERTRE. LITHOGRAPH. C. 1925.

always scenes of streets or houses. Trees are
rare in his paintings, and when there are any
they are the stunted trees that one finds in the
back streets and outskirts of the city. This

uniformity of vision, this continuity of subject and inspiration, helped to bring about the process always to be observed in the great artist— he himself becomes a substitute for nature. In the same way that one says of a fresh young girl with soft pink complexion: "She is a Renoir", so it has become inevitable to say of a deserted street on the city's edge, a white wall with crumbling plaster, a humble little building with red-tiled roof, of a barracks or a village church: "It's a Utrillo."

He began by painting what he saw about him every day—Montmartre where he lived, the outskirts of the city where he often went with his mother. Then, once he had felt his subject deeply within him, once he had really found his style, he no longer needed to work from life. It was sufficient for him to have a postcard for a model so sure he was, by his own miraculous sensitivity, by his sureness of touch, to add to his subject the very atmosphere which would have been communicated to him had the scene been present before him in reality. There from the Butte Montmartre he painted both the dark gloomy quarters of Clignancourt and the rustic scenes and village streets that surround the Place du Tertre. The paint in these pictures is always laid on thickly but uniformly. The houses are almost always drawn with plumb-line accuracy. Carefully preparing the outline of his picture with a ruler, Utrillo sought more and more to obtain perfect regularity and symmetry of line before going on to apply the colours to his drawing with rare sensitivity. Most of the paintings are on cardboard or wooden panels which soak up the heavy mix, thus giving that double effect of thickness and delicacy. Mix is indeed the word, for he prepared his colours as one prepares a sauce, grinding them and stirring them in a bowl, before applying them with a palette-knife to the walls and houses of his paintings. The same subjects reappear time and again—the *Lapin Agile* and its little terrace on the flight of steps in the Rue des Saules with its single tree; the *Bergerie de la Belle Gabrielle*, in the Rue du Mont-Cenis, said to have been a present from Henri IV to Gabrielle d'Estrées; the Place du Tertre, the tiny village square where, in the year he died, Utrillo painted his last picture from nature for a film of Sacha Guitry's on Paris; the little church of Saint Pierre, the oldest church in Paris, with its two pillars that bear testimony of the ancient Roman temple which once crowned the hilltop; and, of course, the Sacré-Cœur itself. This latter subject he painted so many times and from so many angles —from the little streets that surround it, the Rue Norvins, Rue Saint-Éleuthère, Rue du Chevalier-de-la-Barre. The old houses above which the two white domes tower in these paintings are now almost all "cabarets-chantants" or little shops where the tourist may buy art souvenirs or religious trinkets.

After a time Utrillo no longer went down into the street to paint. His subjects he found in the pile of postcards on his table, and clients ordering a painting had only to run through the selection and make their choice. Most of the cards were views of the streets of Paris or the suburbs, but there were also among them streets

STREET IN MONTMARTRE.   LITHOGRAPH.   1952-1953.

MOULIN DE LA GALETTE. LITHOGRAPH. 1925.

of provincial towns in which the artist had never
set foot.

What with the ravages of drink, uncertain
health and failing reason, Utrillo never quite
realized what was happening to his existence.
The fact that his paintings were fetching higher
and higher prices, that he had become famous,

and that people were writing books about him, never seemed to come home to him. He just went on painting, painting, painting, until the day of his death—hardly with full consciousness it seemed, but in a state of secondary awareness. Just after the first World War one of the finest collections of his works ever to be gathered together was shown in a gallery in the Rue La Boétie, but it was only with the greatest difficulty that he could be persuaded to be present at the opening. He walked round looking at his paintings but did not recognize one of them, and was not even aware that they were his work. His life with his mother and with her husband Utter, also a painter, was not always easy or

DEBRAY FARMHOUSE, MONTMARTRE. LITHOGRAPH. 1924.

peaceful, and many a stormy scene shook the walls of the old house in the Rue Cortot. Finally he married and, at the insistence of his wife, Lucie Valore, left Paris to live in a villa at Le Vésinet.

It was only natural that in view of his broken health and his frequent failure to recognize his own authorship of the paintings shown to him, he should become an easy mark for counterfeiters. Imitation Utrillos abound as do imitation Corots. The apparent naïveté of design and simple colour harmonies of his paintings have been copied many and many a time, but the genuine Utrillo can be detected at a glance. The nostalgia and poetic feeling engendered with almost heart-rending intensity by those subdued tones, by those colours matched and juxtaposed with such delicate refinement, by that style so personal and despite its simplicity so inimitable, are unmistakeable. Utrillo died in 1955 at the age of seventy-two, beyond the reach of misery, misfortune and distress, just as he remained beyond the reach of honours and wealth. And in that lies the greatness of the artist, of the great artist.

LIST OF PLATES

14. A CORNER OF OLD MONTMARTRE. LITHO-GRAPH. 1947. *Publisher : Pétridès.*

15. THE RUE DE MONTMARTRE IN WINTER. LITHOGRAPH. 1947. *Publisher : Pétridès.*

Place du Tertre
Montmartre,

Maurice Utrillo V

Maurice Utrillo

Montmartre

Montmartre.   Maurice Utrillo